Thank you, God, for sharing this vision with me
and allowing me to hold the gift to illuminate it.
This book is dedicated to Pastor Alice. She has shown me what it means to give,
and through the light in her spirit she has transformed a community and helped
so many to freedom. God bless you, mama . . . God bless you.

Text copyright © 2011 Shane W. Evans

Illustrations copyright © 2011 by Shane W. Evans

A Neal Porter Book

Published by Roaring Brook Press

Roaring Brook Press is a division of Holtzbrinck Publishing Holdings Limited Partnership

175 Fifth Avenue, New York, New York 10010

www.roaringbrookpress.com

Library of Congress Cataloging-in-Publication Data

Evans, Shane.

Underground / Shane W. Evans. — 1st ed.

p. cm.

"A Neal Porter book."

ISBN 978-1-59643-538-4

1. Underground Railroad—Juvenile literature. 2. Fugitive slaves—United States—History—
19th century—Juvenile literature. 3. Antislavery movements—United States—
History—19th century—Juvenile literature. 4. Abolitionists—United States—
History—19th century—Juvenile literature. I. Title.

E450.E94 2010

973.7'115—dc22

2010007735

Roaring Brook Press books are available for special promotions and premiums.

For details contact: Director of Special Markets, Holtzbrinck Publishers.

First Edition 2011

Book design by Jennifer Browne

Printed in the United States of America by Worzalla, Stevens Point, Wisconsin

5 7 9 8 6 4

The darkness.

The escape.

We run.

We crawl.

We rest.

We make
new friends.

Others help.

Some don't make it.

We are tired.

We are almost there.

The light.

The Sun.

Freedom.

I am free.
He is free. She is free.
We are free.